BOY SCOUTS OF AMERICA
MERIT BADGE SERIES

COMPUTERS

 BOY SCOUTS OF AMERICA®

Requirements

1. Discuss with your counselor the tips for online safety.

2. Give a short history of the computer. Explain how the invention of the computer has affected society and science and technology.

3. Do the following:
   a. Describe four uses of computers outside your home.
   b. Describe three ways you and your family could use a personal computer other than for games and entertainment

4. Explain the following to your counselor:
   a. The five major parts of a computer
   b. How text, sound, pictures, and video files are stored in a computer's memory
   c. How file compression works and how compression affects the quality of the file
   d. Describe two computer chip–based devices, and describe how they are "smarter" because of the chip and its program.

5. Do the following:
   a. Explain what a program or software application is and how it is developed.
   b. Name three programming languages and describe their uses.
   c. Name four software packages you or your family could use, and explain how you would use them.
   d. Discuss ways you can help protect a computer from viruses and how to protect the information stored on a computer.

35878
ISBN 978-0-8395-3246-0
©2009 Boy Scouts of America
2010 Printing

BANG/Brainerd, N
8-2010/0608

e. Describe how computers are linked to generate and access the Internet and the World Wide Web.

Do THREE of the following:

a. Using a spreadsheet program, develop a food budget for a patrol weekend campout.

b. Using a word processor, write a letter to the parents of your troop's Scouts, inviting them to a court of honor.

c. Using a computer graphics program, design and draw a campsite plan for your troop.

d. Using a computer graphics program, create a flier for an upcoming troop event, incorporating both text and some type of visual such as a photograph or illustration.

e. Using an Internet search engine (with your parent's permission), find ideas about how to conduct a troop court of honor or campfire program. Print out a copy of the ideas from at least three different Web sites. Share what you found with your counselor, and explain how you used the search engine to find this information.

f. Using a presentation software program of your choice, develop a report about a topic that has been approved by your counselor. For your presentation, create at least 10 slides.

g. Using a digital camera, take a picture of a troop activity. Transfer the picture file to a computer and use photographic software to make it small enough to send easily as an e-mail attachment. Then, using a computer connected to the Internet (with your parent's permission), send an e-mail to someone you know. In your message, include the photograph as an attachment. Verify that the person received your e-mail and was able to view the attachment.

h. Using a database manager, create a troop roster that includes the name, rank, patrol, and telephone number of each Scout. Show your counselor that you can sort the register by each of the following categories: rank, patrol, and alphabetically by name.

Do ONE of the following:

a. Using a database program of your choice, create a troop roster that can be sorted by the name, rank, patrol, and telephone number of each Scout. Create a form within the database manager to access each Scout's informati individually. Show your counselor how the form works

b. Using a software package of your choice for computer-aided design (CAD), create an engineering-style drawin of a simple object. Include the top, bottom, and at leas one side view and the dimensions.

c. Create a blog and use it as an online journal of your Scouting activities, including group discussions and meetings, campouts, and other events. Your blog shoul have at least five entries and two photographs or illustrations. You need not post the blog to the Internet but you will need to share it with your counselor. If yo decide to go live with your blog, you must first share i with your parents AND counselor and get their approv

d. Create a Web page for your troop, patrol, school, or place of worship. Include at least three articles and twe photographs or illustrations. Your Web page should hav at least one link to a Web site that would be of interes to your audience. You need not post the page to the Internet. However, if you decide to do so, you must first share it with your parents AND counselor and get their approval.

e. Visit a business or an industrial plant that uses compute Observe what tasks the computers accomplish, and be prepared to discuss what you have learned.

8. Explain the following to your counselor:

a. Why copyright laws exist

b. Why it is not permissible to accept a free copy of a pai copyrighted computer game or program from a friend unless the game or program is considered freeware or shareware. Explain the concepts of freeware and sharewa

c. The restrictions and limitations of downloading music from the Internet

9. Find out about three career opportunities in the compute industry. Pick one and find out the education, training, a experience required for this profession. Discuss this with your counselor, and explain why this profession might interest you. Report what you learn to your counselor.

Contents

01100010011110101010100010101101
01011101010000101010100000111010
01010101000010101010001011010110
10101101010010110100101010110101
10100010101111010101010010010011`
01100010011110101010100010101101
01011101010000101010100000111010
01010101000010101010001011010110
10101101010010110100101010110101
10100010101111010101010010010011

Computers in Modern Life

...nply put, *computers* are machines that perform math—adding, ...ptracting, multiplying, and dividing. By performing simple ...culations exceedingly fast, computers can operate robots that ...ild cars, command monitors and printers to display and print ...rds, generate fast-moving video games, and send e-mail ...ssages around the world.

At the heart of every modern computer is the *transistor*, ... electronic switch with two positions: *on* and *off*. These two ...sitions also can be called *yes* and *no*, or *true* and *false*. To ...rform any task, a computer breaks down the job into a series ... yes-or-no questions, such as, "Is someone pushing the 'S' ...y on the keyboard?" If the answer is yes, the computer will ...nd a message to display an **S** on the *monitor*. If the answer ...no, then no action is taken.

Software engineers write sets of instructions for ...mputers called *programs,* which accomplish complex ...ks by performing the computer's simple yes-or-no ...gic millions of times per second. Even though a ...mputer may seem to be thinking, it is actually ...ly doing what a person programmed it to do— ...ry quickly.

In addition to calculating, a computer is ...levice that can process information—for ...ample, your grades in English class, or ...e amount of water your family used ... your home last month— ...cording to a set of ...structions. Many ...mputers can also ...ore information to ... retrieved later.

Italicized terms such as *software* and *program* can be found in the glossary toward the end of this pamphlet.

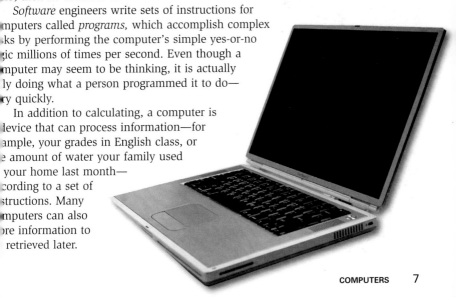

Computers Are Everywhere

Computers are found almost anywhere there are machines or electronic gadgets. Often you can't even see the computers because they are smaller than your fingertip and hidden. Tiny computer processors are built into mobile phones, garage door openers, DVD players, thermostats, digital cameras, remote controls, wristwatches, vehicles, portable radios, and even greeting cards.

As computers become smaller and less expensive, they are used in more ways. Your passport, the little booklet that identifies you when you enter or leave a country, now has an embedded computer chip. Thanks to a computerized tag attached to the car, drivers can pay automatically as they pass through a tollbooth on the highway.

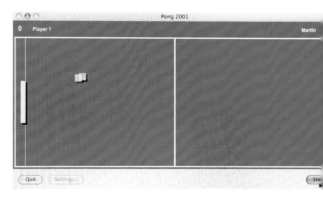

Video games have come a long way since "Pong," an early video game of the 1970s that consisted of simple white blips moving on the screen.

Computers don't just make our lives eas-, safer, and more comfortable. They have come essential to business, industry, sci-ce, medicine, communications—practically ery part of society. For instance, stores can ep just the right amount of products on eir shelves. When you buy a shirt at the partment store, a computer subtracts one irt from the inventory list so the manager n know exactly when his shirt supply is v and it's time to order more shirts. That ves the business money because it keeps e store from having too many shirts on nd—or from having too few.

The worldwide network of computers own as the *Internet* has revolutionized mmunications. Now, instead of waiting ys or even weeks to receive a letter through e postal mail, computer users can type an ctronic letter, or *e-mail,* that zips around e world in seconds. Vast databases of information e available on the *World Wide Web,* allowing students d scientists to research direct from their home or office. ople now shop online for items from books to cars.

In industry, computers have streamlined every step of e production process through computer-aided drafting, sign, engineering, and manufacturing. Computers allow oducts to be conceived, designed, and tested virtually— at is, before they have taken physical form. In this way, car designer can make three-dimensional models of car parts, t" them together, and even test how well they work, all on e computer screen. When it comes time to manufacture e product, computers can also control the machines that nstruct the parts.

Using computers, phone companies keep track of millions of customers, sending each a detailed bill every month showing them precisely which phone numbers they called, how many minutes they talked on the phone, and how much each call cost.

Computers are also common in the entertainment industry. One person using a synthesizer can make music that sounds like a whole orchestra playing. Computers help animators create special effects in movies, such as making superheroes appear to jump from building to building. Computers also drive video games, a business now almost as big as the movie industry.

Handheld GPS (global positioning system) devices use computer and satellite technology to tell hikers or drivers where they are on a map.

Computer technology has completely changed photography.
t a few years ago, most cameras still used film to capture
t. You not only had to buy the film, you also had to pay to
e it processed after the pictures were taken. Today, most
neras are *digital*, with pictures captured electronically and
red on computer chips.

Abacus 1100

Slide rule 161
Mechanical calculator 164
Automatic loom (punch cards) 180

Babbage's computer 1830s
Boolean logic 1850s

Hollerith's electric tabulator 1880
Analog computer 1927
EDVAC 1946
ENIAC 1947

Transistor 1947

Integrated circuit late 1950s
UNIVAC 1951
Microprocessor 1971
Altair 8800 1975
Apple II® 1977
IBM PC 1981

hello.

Macintosh® 1984

The history of computers

History of Computers

...e modern computer reflects the ingenuity of many inventors,
...athematicians, and philosophers working over a period of
...nturies, often improving on the work of others who came
...fore them.

Today, we use handheld electronic calculators at home, school, and work. But another calculating aid, the abacus, has been around since about 1100 B.C. and is still used in some parts of the world. It consists of a wooden frame with beads that slide along rods. By assigning a value to the beads and sliding them up and down the rods, users can add, subtract, multiply, and divide.

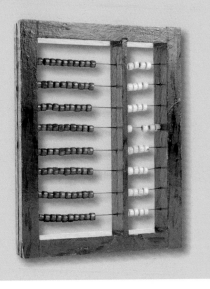

Early Math Aids

In 1617, Scottish mathematician **John Napier** invented an aid to calculation—the concept of logarithms, which simplify the task of multiplying and dividing into a form of addition and subtraction. He inscribed his logarithms on a set of calculating rods he called "Napier's bone: Soon after, an English clergyman named Willia Oughtred invented a device based on Napier's logarithms: the slide rule. It remained in use fo the next 350 years, until the electronic calculate was invented. Like the earlier inventions, howev the slide rule was only an aid to calculation, no a true calculator.

In 1804, a French weaver named **Joseph-Marie Jacquard** invented an automatic loom, or weaving machine, controlled by sets of instructions coded into punched cards. Different cards held instructions for different patterns to be woven into fabrics. The idea of using coded instructions readable by a machine became the basis of computer programs many years later.

First Calculator

The first practical mechanical calculator was invented by a French mathematician. In 1642, while still a teenager, **Blaise Pascal** invented an adding machine called the Pascaline, which worked with wheels and gears. Pascal's father, a tax collector, used the Pascaline to add up how much money people owed the government—something modern computers still do today. In 1670, a German named **Gottfried von Leibniz** improved on Pascal's invention, developing a calculator that not only could add and subtract, but also could multiply and divide.

Blaise Pascal

The First Computer

In the 1830s, English mathematician **Charles Babbage** designed plans for the analytical engine. His machine, intended to automatically produce mathematical tables for navigation at sea, consisted of four main parts, all found in today's computers:

An *input device* to read instructions from punched cards

A *memory* to store the instructions and results

A *processor*, which Babbage called a mill

An *output device* to print the tables of numbers

Babbage's analytical engine could be programmed to perform different tasks. That feature also made it like a modern computer—although the analytical engine was completely mechanical and powered by steam, not electricity. **Augusta Ada King,** who wrote a program for the analytical engine, is considered to be the world's first computer programmer. Unfortunately, Babbage was never able to complete the machine or test it. A model of his earlier design, the difference engine, was finally built at London's Science Museum for display in 1991. It had 4,000 parts and weighed three tons.

Augusta Ada King

In the 1840s and 1850s, English mathematician and philosopher **George Boole** developed a kind of logic that allows thoughts to be expressed in mathlike terms. The basic forms of Boolean logic (also called Boolean algebra) are the AND, OR, and NOT operations.

George Boole

- An AND operation is one in which two or more conditions must be true to achieve a result. For example, before you can safely cross a street intersection, the walk sign must be lit AND cross traffic must be stopped.

- In an OR operation, the result will happen if either condition is met: If it is cold outside OR if it is raining, you will put on a jacket before leaving the house.

- With a NOT operation, a result happens when a particular condition is not met: You will go to school if today does NOT fall on the weekend.

Years after Boole died, computer designers arranged electric switches to perform these operations in what became known as logic circuits, allowing digital computers to mimic human thought processes. Later still, Boolean logic would be used in Internet search engines and in specialized languages used to manage data in databases.

dison's Vacuum Tube

1883, a few years after **Thomas lison** invented the electric lightbulb, noticed something peculiar about w electricity flowed inside it. To otect the brightly glowing filament, had been removed from the bulb, eating a vacuum tube. Surprisingly, he placed a metal plate inside the ilb, electricity would flow across the icuum from the filament to the plate. lison patented the discovery of how ectrons flowed across a vacuum, now iown as the Edison Effect, though he ade little use of it.

In 1906, American inventor e de Forest discovered that placing iree electrodes inside the bulb created i amplifier. In addition to making dio and television possible, this icuum tube could also serve as an ttremely fast on-and-off switch. This scovery would prove crucial in the evelopment of digital computers.

Thomas Edison

pecial-Purpose Calculators

very 10 years, the U.S. government conducts a census, or study, collect information about everyone who lives in the country. y 1880, the population was so large—over 49 million—that ie task took seven years to complete. To speed things up for ie 1890 census, the government turned to American inventor erman Hollerith. His electric tabulating machine automatically corded punched cards prepared for every individual. The cards eld information that could be presented in different ways— ir example, to find out how many married people lived in

Herman Hollerith, the father of automated data processing, formed a company that would later become the giant IBM corporation.

Tennessee, or how many owned farms smaller than 3 acres. This machine was the beginning of automated data processing.

Soon, other companies were formed to build *special-purpose calculating machines* to help businesses. Eventually, universities joined in, finding scientific and military uses for the technology. These machines were one of a kind, and each had its peculiarities

WHAT'S WHAT: THE WHATCHAMACALLIT THING

Punched card

Massachusetts Institute of Technology engineer Vannevar Bush invented the differential analyzer, an electromechanical analog computer, in 1927.

e U.S. military used first-generation digital computers like this ENIAC to calculate jectories of artillery shells and to help build weapons.

At Harvard University, professor **Howard Aiken** worked the Mark I using electromagnetic relays as switches. At e University of Pennsylvania, **John William Mauchly** and **Presper Eckert Jr.** designed the EDVAC and the ENIAC, ing vacuum tubes as switches, which worked a thousand nes faster than the relays in the Mark I. The military used ese "first generation" digital computers to calculate weapon jectories and help build atomic bombs. Each of these comters weighed tons, filled an entire room, and consumed ough electricity to light up a small town. They also required ousands of vacuum tubes, which tended to overheat and rn out, needing to be replaced often.

Grace Hopper coined the term "bug" for a computer fault. The original bug was a moth that created a hardware problem in the Mark I. Hopper was the first person to "debug" a computer.

The "Universal" Computer

The first commercially built computer was Mauchly's and Ecke
UNIVAC. It was designed to be a general-purpose, or "universa
computer that would serve scientists, businessmen, and
engineers alike.

The UNIVAC was a *stored-program* computer, meaning
the program didn't have to be fed into the computer as it
was running. Another innovation in the UNIVAC was its abili
to take input from data on magnetic tape, rather than from
punched cards. This ability made it faster and easier to opera
Customers for the new computer—which cost about $1 millic
in the early 1950s—included the U.S. Census Bureau, the Air
Force, and insurance companies.

The Transistor—A Major Breakthrough

Silicon is the most widely used semiconductor material.

In 1947, engineers **John Bardeen, Walter Brattain,** and
William Shockley at Bell Laboratories ushered in the second
generation of computers by inventing the transistor. Like a va
uum tube, the transistor had three terminals. It could functio
as an amplifier and a switch, but it was much smaller, used f
less power, and performed thousands of times faster. It was
made of a solid material known as a *semiconductor,* which
moves electricity more slowly than a conductor and does not
get hot like vacuum tubes.

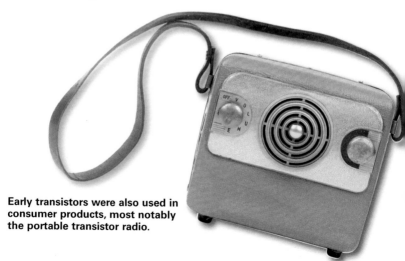

**Early transistors were also used in
consumer products, most notably
the portable transistor radio.**

The Integrated Circuit— An Even Bigger Breakthrough

A major limitation of transistors was that they had to be connected to other electronic components (resistors, capacitors, and diodes) to form circuits. An early computer may have had tens of thousands of transistors and other components that required tens of thousands of hand-soldered connections.

This problem was solved in the late 1950s when **Jack Kilby** of Texas Instruments and, a few months later, **Robert Noyce** of Fairchild Semiconductor, thought of the *integrated circuit*. The concept was simple: Instead of connecting components after they are made, manufacture them all on the same chip of silicon, with built-in connections. The integrated circuit, also called the *microchip*, revolutionized computing. It also made possible such products as the hand-held calculator and the digital wristwatch. Integrated circuits were also used in *minicomputers,* which, though smaller than the big mainframes of the day, still cost tens of thousands of dollars each.

The Apollo space program of the 1960s, with a mission to put an American on the moon by the end of the decade, was an early user of integrated circuits.

The Microprocessor

In 1971, engineers at Intel Corporation, founded by Noyce, advanced the integrated circuit to a new level: They designed the first *microprocessor*, putting all the circuits needed for a computer's *central processing unit* (its "brain," which could run coded instructions) onto a single chip. This invention made the personal computer possible.

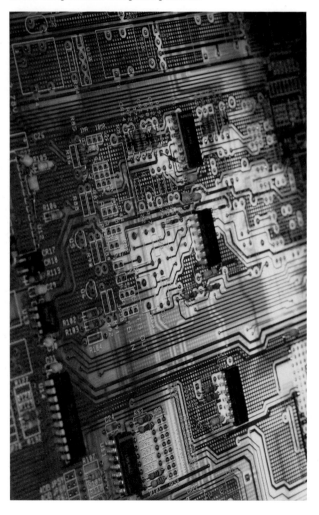

ersonal Computers

The Altair 8800 was an early model *personal* mputer sold in 1975 as a mail-order kit for bbyists to build themselves. That year, yhood chums **Bill Gates** and **Paul Allen,** ong with **Monte Davidoff,** wrote a programing language called BASIC that would run on e Altair. For a fee, they licensed the program the computer maker and formed their own mpany, Microsoft.

Meanwhile, two other young friends, **Steve ozniak** and **Steve Jobs,** were busy working n the Apple II, a personal computer released in 977 by their new company, Apple. Unlike most omputers, the Apple II had color graphics. nis asset made it a good platform for games, nd it became extremely popular with home users.

Apple II

he Altair 8800

The year before, Wozniak and Jobs had worked together making a video game for Atari, a company founded by *Nolan Bushnell*. Atari had already become successful by selling a console that played one video game—called "Pong"—in both arcade and home versions. Pong was the beginning of the multibillion-dollar video game industry.

In 1979, **Daniel Bricklin** and **Robert Frankston** created a software program for the Apple II called VisiCalc, short for "visible calculator." The program automatically calculated rows and columns of numbers arranged in a form known as a *spreadsheet*. This program, which was not available for mainframe computers, helped start a trend of companies installing personal computers in the workplace.

Two years later, IBM introduced its PC (or *personal computer*) based on the Intel 8088 microprocessor. The PC ran its own version of VisiCalc as well as other software programs including a word processor. IBM contracted with Microsoft to supply a form of BASIC for the new computer, as well as an *operating system*, the program that gets the computer up and running, and then interacts with application programs.

Microsoft later created a similar operating system, MS-DOS, for use on computers made by many different companies. The IBM PC and other computers using the MS-DOS platform dominated the business and home computer markets, helping make Microsoft one of the world's largest corporations.

Apple's Macintosh computer also had an important impact on the industry. Introduced in 1984, the Mac's operating system featured a number of innovations that made computers easier to use, many of which had been developed years earlier by researchers working for Xerox. These included a handheld pointing device, or *mouse;* the use of little pictures called *icons* to represent programs and files on the computer screen; and a system of pull-down menus and movable screen displays called windows.

Despite the Macintosh innovations, the PC grew ever more popular, in part because IBM allowed other companies to sell inexpensive "clones" of its PC design, while Apple did not. By 1990, Microsoft managed to incorporate many user-friendly advantages of the Macintosh into the latest version of its operating system, called Windows.

Computers continue to drop in price and grow in power, much as they have throughout their history. In 1971, a microprocessor held 2,250 transistors; by 1993, it was 3.1 million. In early 2008, Intel announced the creation of the first microprocessor to hold two billion transistors. Experts say this exponential growth in computing power cannot continue indefinitely.

As for price, the original IBM PC cost $3,000 when it debuted in 1981, equal to around $7,200 in 2008 (adjusted for inflation). Yet, in 2008, a consumer could buy a desktop PC many times more powerful than the original PC for less than $500.

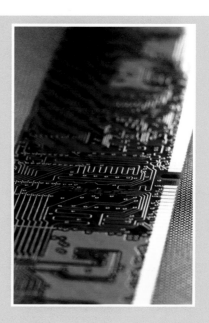

Computers in Your Hand

Rapid increases in computing power have allowed computers to get ever smaller. The early years of this new century have included an explosion in handheld computing devices—not just calculators, but also GPS units, which people now commonly use to find their way while driving; and *personal digital assistants (PDAs)*, small computers you can put in your pocket that can be used as portable media players, electronic address books, mobile phones, and Web *browsers*.

Likewise, enhanced cell phones, called "smart phones," do many tasks beyond making phone calls, including taking pictures, doing calculations, browsing the Internet, handling e-mail, and storing information. Another category of handheld computer is the personal translator. These small, inexpensive devices act like a "speaking dictionary," so you can hear how to pronounce words and phrases in various languages and see how they are spelled on a display screen.

New software programs are continually introduced to take advantage of the increased power and to expand the ways in which we use computers.

The Web Is Born

The 1990s brought another significant revolution: the rapid expansion of the Internet and the World Wide Web, linking computers around the globe and changing the way people communicate and do business. Today, many activities we used to do in person can be done by connecting our computers at home to distant computers called *servers*. By connecting to a server at the bank, for example, we can transfer money from one account to another or pay bills; by connecting to the server at the library, we can renew a book we checked out; by connecting to a server at an online store, we can order all manner of products without ever leaving home. Students now check assignments due and turn in homework online through a Web site kept by their schools or teachers. There are online colleges that grant degrees for work done through the Internet.

See "The Internet and the World Wide Web" later in this pamphlet for more on the Internet and the World Wide Web.

Cloud Computing

What do you get when you combine advances in software with advances in Internet connectivity? Cloud computing. The term refers to the "cloud" of powerful computers called servers scattered throughout the Internet. Increasingly, these servers provide "temporary" software that can be used on computers at home. The software exists on a distant "cloud" and is loaded into the home computer's Web browser only temporarily, while being used.

One example of cloud computing is the picture-editing software that resides on the Web site *http://www.photoshop.com.* Computer users at home can visit the site, upload photographs, and edit them (say, making them sharper or more colorful) without actually downloading any software. An auxiliary program that temporarily loads into the home computer's Web browser makes this possible.

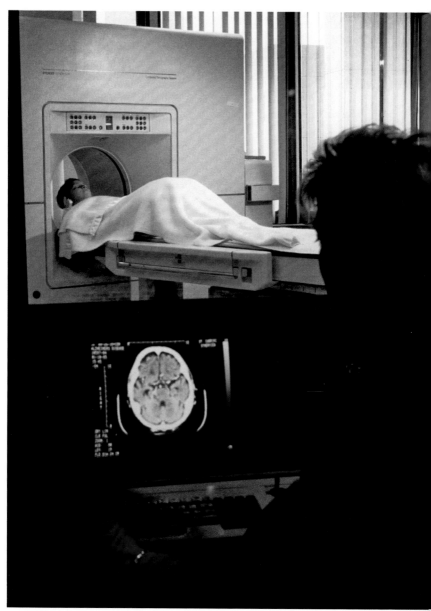

An MRI (Magnetic Resonance Imaging) machine

Types of Computers

There are two basic categories of computers, *special purpose* and *general purpose*.

Special-Purpose Computers

Special-purpose computers are programmed to perform a specific task. Video game consoles—such as the Wii, PlayStation, Xbox, and others—are a form of special-purpose computer. Their special purpose is to play games.

A common type of special-purpose computer is the *embedded computer,* usually found inside a larger device. Embedded computers operate antilock brakes in an automobile, keep time in a digital watch, and organize songs in a digital music player. As computer chips have become smaller and less expensive, more products have been embedded with computers—everything from sewing machines to greeting cards, which will automatically play a tune when you open them. Embedded computers are becoming inexpensive and common enough to be considered disposable.

In many cases, these tiny computers add a level of "intelligence" to the product or device. Computer chips in cell phones, for example, can be programmed not only to store the names and phone numbers of your friends, but also to sound a different ring when each of your friends calls. This lets you know who is calling by the ring alone.

General-Purpose Computers

General-purpose computers, like a PC, can be programmed to perform a wide range of tasks—writing, drawing, editing photographs, social networking, budgeting, playing games, browsing the Internet, and using e-mail. Personal computers come in a variety of shapes and sizes, including desktop, notebook (a portable computer, ideal for browsing the Internet and sending e-mail), tablet, and handheld.

Industry experts predict that handheld computers will become increasingly powerful and may increasingly be used in place of desktop or laptop computers. In fact, some people watch movies and television shows on their cell phones while commuting to work on the subway. With the new *third generation (3G)* technology for mobile networking (communication by portable device), such activities may become commonplace.

An older term for personal computers is *microcomputers.* This term was used to contrast personal computers with larger general-purpose computers, namely, *minicomputers, workstations, mainframe* computers, and *supercomputers.* Although today's small computers are more powerful than the largest computers of years past, and these terms have become less meaningful, they should still be understood.

Supercomputers are the largest, most expensive, and fastest computers available, typically used for tasks involving complex calculations, such as weather forecasting, military weapons simulations, and plotting the motions of galaxies. At this writing, the fastest supercomputer is the IBM Roadrunner, built for the U.S. Department of Energy and housed at the Los Alamos National Laboratory in New Mexico. The Roadrunner's computational speed has been clocked at over 1.026 *quadrillion* (or thousand trillion) calculations per second, making it the first computer to break the speed of one *petaflop.* ("FLOP" stands for FLoating-Point OPerations.) This military computer can simulate nuclear explosions. It may also be used for civilian tasks, such as automobile design.

Mainframes—large computers often used by hundreds or ~~e~~n thousands of different people at once—can run different ~~pr~~ograms at the same time. They are usually connected to ~~ter~~minals (consisting of a monitor and keyboard) that allow a ~~pe~~rson to enter information and retrieve it from the computer. ~~Ma~~inframe computers have traditionally been used for large-~~sc~~ale data processing, such as a company keeping track of ~~mi~~llions of customer accounts.

Smaller than mainframes, *minicomputers* were often used ~~by~~ medium-sized companies to run their manufacturing plants ~~and~~ to keep track of inventories. These were operated as small ~~ma~~inframes, with multiple users. *Workstations* were powerful ~~de~~sktop computers often used by engineers, scientists, graphic ~~art~~ists, moviemakers, and other professionals who use special ~~so~~ftware requiring high-speed processors. These were typically ~~mo~~re powerful than microcomputers.

Today's microcomputers are powerful enough to do much ~~of~~ the work that was once done by minicomputers and even ~~ma~~inframes. Some companies that would have used a main-~~fra~~me or minicomputer in the past can now use a *client-server* ~~ar~~rangement instead. This allows numerous microcomputers ~~to~~ be connected via a network with access to files or programs ~~sto~~red on one or more shared microcomputers known as ~~ser~~vers. Servers are categorized by the type of work they do ~~an~~d can include file servers, application servers, mail servers, ~~an~~d Web servers, which hold the files that are displayed on ~~Int~~ernet Web pages.

~~Pe~~rsonal digital assistants, or PDAs, are handheld microcomputers ~~th~~at use either a stylus and touch screen or a tiny keyboard for input.

Parts of a Computer

Every general-purpose computer—from large multiuser systems to a handheld one—is made up of the same main elements: a central processor, input devices, storage units, and output devices.

Central Processor

The "brain" of the computer is the *central processing unit* (CPU). This part stores information that is put into the computer, performs operations on that information, and creates output based on the results. The CPU may be a single chip made of silicon that has millions of tiny circuits built into it. The CPU in a personal computer is usually located on the main circuit board, or *motherboard*, which is like the foundation to a house. The most important components in the computer connect to it.

The speed of early microprocessors was measured in thousands of cycles per second, or kilohertz (kHz); then came measurement in millions of cycles per second, or megahertz (MHz). More recent models have been measured in billions of cycles per second, or gigahertz (GHz). This measurement, called a computer's "clock speed," is only one factor that affects actual performance. A better test is in how quickly a computer runs application programs.

Collectively, the various computer chips that perform critical functions are known as the chipset.

Most computers have *coprocessors* to help the CPU, for example, to enhance the graphics and sound capabilities of the computer without slowing down other functions.

The *cursor* is a blinking line that shows where on the screen the next character you type will appear.

MEMORY

One component connected to the motherboard is memory. There are two main types of memory: *ROM* (read-only memory) and *RAM* (random-access memory).

ROM is permanent memory that remains in place even when the computer is turned off. Data stored in ROM cannot be changed. Information stored in ROM is "maintained" in *BIOS* (Basic Input-Output System), a small program that starts—or boots—the computer, checks its components, and launches the operating system.

RAM is temporary memory. When you launch an application program, it is loaded into RAM. So is information that you put into the computer during a particular work session. RAM remembers this information only while the computer is turned on. If you turn off the computer, everything in RAM is lost. The exception to this is *flash RAM,* a type of memory that retains data after the device is turned off. Flash memory chips are found in digital cameras, handheld computers, cell phones, and other devices.

CONTROLLERS AND PORTS

In addition to memory, you often find on the motherboard a graphics controller, a disk controller, expansion slots, and several ports. A graphics controller tells the monitor how to display information on the screen. A disk controller tells a removable disk or hard disk how to store information for later use.

Ports are connectors that allow you to attach any number of things—monitor, printer, modem, mouse, or keyboard—to the computer. Many computers use the same *USB* (universal serial bus) ports for connecting *peripheral* devices. Another type of high-speed port is the *FireWire* (or IEEE 1394) port, often used to transfer large files such as video footage to, or from, the computer.

put Devices

ne *keyboard* is used to type char-
ters into the computer and move
ings around on the screen.
omputer keyboards typically have
ecial keys not found on a type-
riter, including a row of *function*
eys across the top that can be
ogrammed to do different tasks
nd a set of arrow keys that allows
ou to move the *cursor* around
le screen.

Most keyboards use the standard QWERTY key layout. Designed during the 19th century to separate certain letter combinations to help keep mechanical typewriters from jamming, the QWERTY layout is named for the order of the letters, reading from the left, on the top row of alphabet keys.

A *mouse* is another device used to input information into a computer. It may have a roller ball with two wheels that sense the direction in which the mouse is being dragged across the desktop or mouse pad. Or, if the mouse is *optical,* it will use a small *LED* (light-emitting diode) that bounces light off the desktop into a sensor that detects the mouse's position. By pointing to different parts of the screen, an on-screen cursor controlled by a mouse can select different features.

Sound digitizers are used to convert sounds we can hear, such as voices or music, into a form that can be understood by the computer. Some computers are equipped with microphones so that you can record directly onto your computer. The microphone connects to a *sound card,* which holds the circuitry for recording and reproducing sound. A sound card usually has an input jack to receive signals from a microphone or an external music source such as a CD player, and it connects to jacks into which you can plug speakers and headphones.

A *scanner* is a device that converts printed words or pictures into a digital form that can be saved on the computer as a file. An *optical character recognition* program can convert the words into a form that can be edited on the computer. A scanned picture image can be manipulated with graphics software.

A *sensor* is an input device that can be used to check physical conditions such as temperature, light, pressure, magnetism, motion, and moisture. The sensor *reads* and converts the information into a digital format so that the computer can understand it. Sensors are used in scientific laboratories to track experiments, and in manufacturing to guide robots and their movements. In digital cameras, a special light-sensing computer chip converts photons into digital impulses.

orage Units

rage units save information and programs for later use,
n when the computer is turned off. Most storage is either
gnetic or optical. A third type, *flash* memory, holds data
nonvolatile computer chips that retain data even without
stant electric power.

Magnetic memory works much like audiotape or videotape.
e disk material is coated with tiny particles that will hold a
gnetic charge. When a file is stored on the disk, a pattern of
sitive and negative particles is created. The computer's disk
ve reads these charged particles to interpret the file; it can
o change the charge of the particle by *writing* to the disk.

Magnetic storage is usually in the form of a *removable hard
k,* or *tape drive.* Hard disks can either be fixed inside a PC
some other device, such as a portable music player, or can
made as removable cartridges. As technology improves,
rd-drive capacity continually grows while the physical size
hard drives shrinks.

Mostly a thing of the past,
a diskette is another form
of magnetic storage. The
diskette consists of a thin
film disk inside a hard
plastic case. Easily inserted
and removed from the
computer, a diskette could
be used for transferring
text files from one com-
puter to another. Today,
its capacity is too limited
to be of much use in transferring larger files such
as photographs, music,
or programs.

> Early hard disks held only 10 megabytes of information,
> or about 10 minutes of music.

A hard disk is made up of a series of stacked, rigid (hard)
circular disks, or platters, that spin on a thin cushion of air at
up to 15,000 revolutions a minute. Each platter in the hard disk
has its own *read/write arm* that moves across the surface like
the arm on a phonograph record. But instead of a needle, the
read/write arm contains a *read/write head* that transfers data
to and from the disk.

Information on hard disks is organized in *tracks*—concentric circles almost like grooves on a phonograph record—and *sectors*, shaped like pieces of a pie. On a single track, two or more sectors together make up a *cluster*. A file that you save to the disk—say, a book report, photograph, or song recording—may be scattered across hundreds of different clusters. Not to worry. The disk keeps a type of directory that tells the computer which clusters hold the pieces it needs to assemble the complete file. Because it does not have to search the entire disk, the computer finds the information quickly.

Flash memory is now commonly used in a portable pocket-size device called a flash drive or thumb drive. It consists of a circuit board housed inside a plastic case and uses a USB plug to connect to your computer or other device. At this writing, flash drive capacity ranges from about 64 megabytes to 64 gigabytes.

Using portable devices like a USB flash drive allow the user to take any number of files on the go.

A tape drive uses a cartridge with a long piece of magnetic tape wound inside it. The cartridge head reads or writes the information on the tape as the tape passes over it. A tape drive can only read tape from beginning to end—it cannot jump around at random the way a disk drive reads a disk. This makes tape drives slow at accessing information, which is why most are used only for backing up information in case the computer is lost or damaged.

Optical storage devices can hold very large amounts of information, and the disks are relatively inexpensive. *CD-ROM* (compact disc read-only memory) and *DVD-ROM* (digital video disc read-only memory) are examples of optical storage. With these devices, information is stored using a laser rather than magnetically (just as with a CD player). A laser burns tiny pits into the surface of a disc. The flat areas between pits are called lands. The laser can later read these pits and lands as binary code.

The following table compares the typical storage capability of different media:

Medium	Typical Capacity	Equivalent Size
High-density diskette	1.4 megabytes	720 typed pages or 80 seconds of music
Zip disk	100 to 750 megabytes	50,000 typed pages or 1.6 hours of music
CD-ROM	700 megabytes	350,000 typed pages or 11 hours of music
DVD (standard, single layer)	4.7 gigabytes	2.35 million typed pages, 78 hours of music, or 2.16 hours of standard-definition video
DVD (Blu-ray, single layer)	25 gigabytes	415 hours of music or 11.5 hours of video
Portable USB flash drive	64 gigabytes	1,062 hours of music or 29 hours of video
Portable hard drive	1 terabyte	16,593 hours of music or 453 hours of video
Fixed hard drive	1.5 terabytes	24,889 hours of music or 679 hours of video

Output Devices

The *monitor* allows you to see the output of the computer. A monitor displays information by using *pixels,* short for picture elements. A pixel is a single dot on the screen. Groups of pixels form text or pictures on the screen. A monitor can have different *resolutions*—the more pixels it can show, the higher its resolution and the sharper the picture. A monitor described as 1,280 x 1,024 resolution can display 1,280 pixels across and 1,024 up and down, a total of 1,310,720 pixels at one time.

Monitors can display information in black and white *(monochrome),* shades of gray, or color. Monitors can be a *CRT* (cathode-ray tube) or an *LCD* (liquid-crystal display), also known as a *flat-screen* or *flat-panel* monitor. A CRT, the older form of monitor, is bulkier, heavier, uses more energy than an LCD, and is steadily becoming obsolete.

Notice that monitors can have different rectangular shapes, or *aspect ratios.* The standard monitor ratio in width to height is 4:3, meaning the monitor is slightly wider than it is tall. (Most digital cameras shoot pictures with this same ratio in order to match the monitor.) Newer monitors may have a wider format, 16:9, which is the shape of high-definition television.

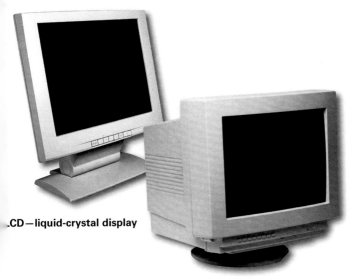

LCD—liquid-crystal display

CRT—cathode-ray tube

A *sound card,* described earlier as an input device, also functions as an output device. It takes sound (stored in digital form that computers understand) and converts it to analog form. Once the sound is converted, it is sent to a speaker either inside the computer or attached to it, which generates the sound that you hear. It might also output sound to a jack in which you can plug headphones for listening.

A *printer* allows you to print out text and images on paper. Several characteristics determine a printer's quality: how sharply and quickly it can print; the quantity and variety of paper it can hold; and, in the case of a color printer, how true its color reproduction. Generally speaking, sharpness (or *resolution*) of 300 DPI (dots per inch) is adequate for printing text. This means a solid one-inch printed square would consist of 90,000 tiny dots (300 across by 300 down). A resolution of 600 DPI renders higher-quality text and good graphics. For photographic-quality images, resolutions of 1,200 or even 2,400 DPI are common.

The most common print technology used with personal computers are laser printers and ink-jet printers. Other types include thermal printers, impact printers, plotters, and multifunction printers.

onnecting Devices

vices used to connect computers to one another can be nsidered both input and output devices. *Ethernet* is the most mmon technology for connecting computers in a local area work; typically, computers are located in the same building. ch computer in the network has an Ethernet card and plugs o the network with a cable.

For connecting distant computers, a *modem,* short for 10dulator demodulator," is required. A standard modem ows you to communicate with other computers over a ephone line. Modems convert information from a form at a computer understands to a form that can travel over a ephone line. Once information gets to the computer on the 1er end of the line, it is converted by another modem back to a form that it can understand. Modems are used to provide 1at is commonly called a "dial-up" connection to the Internet.

> Standard modems send data at speeds up to
> 56 kilobits per second.

Faster modem connections, known as *broadband,* are quickly replacing most dial-up connections. Typically, they deliver data at speeds from 256 kilobits up to 50 megabits per second—or five to 100 times faster than the fastest dial-up. *DSL* (digital subscriber line) technology uses the same copper telephone lines as a standard modem, but because DSL produces a higher-frequency signal than voice communications, you can transfer data and chat with a friend over the same phone line at the same time.

A *cable modem* uses the same coaxial cable that brings cable TV signals into your home. *Optical fiber* uses light rays to transmit data through plastic or glass fibers bundled into cables, potentially at higher rates of speed than coaxial cable. A *satellite Internet* connection is beamed from an orbiting satellite to a dish mounted onsite and transferred by cable to your computer. It is commonly used to bring broadband access to rural areas where DSL, coaxial cable, and fiber-optic cable aren't available.

Broadband connections can be fast enough to "stream" news, music, games, and video. That means you can hear or view the data while it is being received rather than having to wait for it to be downloaded first.

Wi-Fi (wireless fidelity) is a way of connecting your computer to the Internet wirelessly over a short distance. Typically, you connect a base station or *router* to your DSL, cable, or satellite modem. Then you add a special "wireless" card to your laptop computer or desktop computer located in another room in the house. (Most computers now come with Wi-Fi capability built in.) The card receives radio signals sent out from the router, establishing your Internet connection over the airwaves. Increasingly, coffee shops, airports, and other businesses are setting up "hot spots" where customers with Wi-Fi-equipped portable computers can conveniently connect to the Internet.

Understanding Data and Files

Information stored on your computer is called *data.* You may have used an input device to enter data, such as a keyboard to type in a list of names. Or the computer may have created the data as output—for example, a word-processing program used to create address labels by merging a list of names with street addresses from a second list.

Almost all data is stored in the form of *files.* There are many different types of files, including number, text, picture, sound, and video files. Software programs such as database programs may create special types of files, each one saved or stored on a computer under a different *file name.* The type, or *format,* of the file is identified by the suffix, or *extension*—usually several letters long—that follows a dot after the file name. For example, in the file name *badgerpatrol. txt,* the ".txt" indicates that this is a text file.

What Extension, Please?

It is important to use the correct extension when creating a file name, particularly if the file will be e-mailed to another computer or viewed on a Web page. If the servers that display Web pages or help send e-mail can't read those extensions, they can't tell the receiving computer what sort of file it is receiving—and the recipient won't be able to process the file.

There are thousands of different types of files and file extensions. Some can be read only by a specific brand of computer. However, many popular file formats can now be read on either operating system so long as the computer is running the required software.

Extension	File Type
Text files	
.txt	ASCII text
.doc	Microsoft Word® (word processing)
Image files	
.jpg	Popular for saving photographs; adjustable compression ratio to achieve exact desired file size
.gif	Nonphotographic images such as icons, buttons, drawings, and figures
.png	Image format with better color reproduction than .gif
.bmp	Short for bitmap, a standard Windows® graphics format
.tif	Offers a lossless way to compress graphics; produces much larger file than .jpg
Sound files	
.mp3	High compression of sound data with only a slight loss in quality
.aiff, .au	Macintosh®-platform sound file
.wav	Windows®-platform sound file
.aac, .wma	High compression; even better quality than .mp3 file
Video files	
.avi	Windows® video file
.mov, .mpg, .mpeg	Movie file in Mac® or Windows® platform

Storing Data

Let's look at some main types of data and how they are stored
on the computer.

Numbers

Think of your computer as a collection of billions of circuits,
each with just two positions, off and on. These two positions
are represented by the numerals 0 and 1, which make up the
binary number system. All data is stored in the computer as
groups of 0s and 1s. Each individual numeral is called a *bit,*
short for binary digit. Bits are clumped in larger groups, usually
of eight bits each, called *bytes.* Each byte represents a number
or letter.

Binary numbers do not look much like the decimal
numbers we are used to seeing. For example, written
as a binary number, the decimal numeral 9 is
00001001. Binary numbers make up **machine code,**
the low-level language that computers translate all
data into before performing operations on it.

Text

Text is stored using a special code corresponding to the numbers between 0 and 255. The code is called *ASCII* (American Standard Code for Information Interchange). Similar to the way it stores decimal numbers, the computer represents each text character as a single byte of information. For example, the letter A is assigned the number 65 in ASCII code, which is 01000001 in binary form. ASCII text is stored without any formatting, such as indentations or boldface.

An ASCII text file is often referred to as a plain text file and can be read by almost any word-processing program. Depending on the program, you can add formatting and save the text in another format.

Pictures

Pictures are stored as a series of small dots called pixels. A monitor might display, for example, 1,024 x 768 pixels; each horizontal row contains 1,024 pixels, and there are 768 rows stacked vertically. In a black-and-white monitor, each pixel requires only one bit of information, telling it to display either 1 (black) or 0 (white). A *grayscale* monitor designates up to 256 different shades of gray between black and white for each pixel.

A color monitor picture displays pixels with three color components—red, green, and blue. Different colors, displayed in various shades and strengths, produce the desired final color. Eight bits of information per pixel will produce 256 different colors on the screen; 16 bits will produce 32,767 colors; and 24 bits will produce 16.7 million colors—the maximum number the human eye can see, sometimes called *true color*.

COMPRESSION

Picture, or image, files are stored in many different formats. Some formats *compress* the picture so that the file takes up less disk space and is easier to e-mail or display on the Web. Many picture formats use *lossy* compression, in which some data is lost forever. Another type of compression, called *lossless,* can temporarily shrink a file by removing parts that are repeated and then, later, restore the file to its full size. Lossless compression is often used with text files and database files.

Sound

Sound is made up of vibrations that travel through the air by passing from one molecule to the next. These vibrations are called waves—if you could see them, they would look like the waves at the beach. The height, or *amplitude,* of the wave determines the volume, or how loud the sound is. How close together the waves are determines the *frequency,* or pitch—how high or low the sound is to your ear.

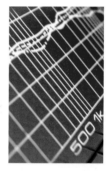

A computer "hears" through a microphone or CD player, via an *analog* signal consisting of these sound waves. The computer sound card feeds this signal through an analog-to-digital converter chip that converts the signal into bits that the computer can read and save as a digital file. As you replay the file, the data is sent through a digital-to-analog converter chip, which rebuilds the shape of the wave and sends that information to the speakers, which vibrate the air, re-creating the original sound wave that you can hear.

Video

Faster microprocessors have made it possible for computers to display moving pictures. Today's computers can store entire movies on their hard drives, including home movies shot with digital video cameras. Digital video, even when compressed, uses up enormous amounts of storage space. As hard drives get larger, more and more people will use their computers to store and edit their video collections.

All computers, including this industrial equipment used in a textile factory, require software to function.

Computer Software

Software, a set of instructions organized into a program, is what makes hardware work. A software program tells the computer specifically what to do. There are three main categories of programs: *operating systems, application programs,* and *programming languages.* Operating systems control the basic operations of the computer. Application programs allow you to do a specific task with the computer, such as write a letter or touch up a photograph. Programming languages are used to write other programs.

Programming languages are used to write other programs.

Operating Systems

Operating system (OS) software is the foundation software on which all other programs run. This set of programs controls all of the computer's basic operations. In the case of personal computers, this includes accepting input from the keyboard, displaying output on the monitor, keeping track of files and directories on the hard drive, and controlling peripheral devices such as disk burners, printers, scanners, speakers, and the mouse.

Because of the work done by the OS, programmers who create application software don't have to write code into their applications to control these basic functions. Likewise, the OS manages upgrades to a computer's hardware (for example, installing more RAM), automatically updating settings in the rest of the system. Another task of the OS is to serve as a kind of traffic cop, allocating processing power and memory space among the various programs that might be running at once while holding back some resources for use by the OS itself.

The most common operating systems are the Windows series (the latest is Windows Vista), the Macintosh series (its latest is OS X), and the UNIX family of operating systems, which includes freeware and inexpensive versions of what is known as Linux.

Applications

As computers become more powerful, and as people think up new ways that computers can help us at school, work, and home, new application programs are continually being written. There is no limit to how many applications can exist. The following are some of the most popular types of application programs, but there are many others adapted to very special needs in science, business, and industry.

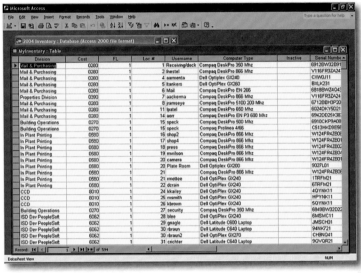

Database manager program

A troop attendance database could be set up with a record for each Scout in the troop. Each record would consist of fields for the Scout's name, patrol, and rank, and for troop meetings, campouts, and other events. An entry of **present** or **absent** could be made in the appropriate field of each Scout's record after each activity. The Scoutmaster could easily see who attended a particular event. The DBM program could also calculate the percentage of participation for each activity. A good DBM can perform complicated sorts and searches of the database and produce neatly printed reports with graphs and charts.

Database managers (DBMs) are used for organizing, storing, and keeping track of a set of information called a *database.* The data are organized in lines called *records,* with each record consisting of a number of *fields.* For each new record, the same set of fields, with different contents in each field, is stored.

Spreadsheets are among the first and most useful programs developed for the personal computer. A spreadsheet performs arithmetic on numbers, which are arranged in rows and columns. The rows and columns intersect to form boxes, which are called *cells.* A *formula* is a function performed on numbers in particular cells—for example, adding the number in cell A1 to the number in cell A2, and having the sum appear in cell A3.

The magic of a spreadsheet is that if you change a number in one cell, the program immediately recalculates the totals in the other cells that are affected by your change. This allows you to perform "what if?" operations. For example, you can figure out how many more Scouts could go to summer camp if the troop raised an additional $300 or $400 at car washes.

In addition to numbers, in a spreadsheet you can also type words, such as headings, names, and explanatory notes. Spreadsheets are surprisingly versatile in the types of reports they can generate. Some examples are fund-raising reports, fitness logs, sports team records, travel budgets, currency conversions, and worksheets for car loans.

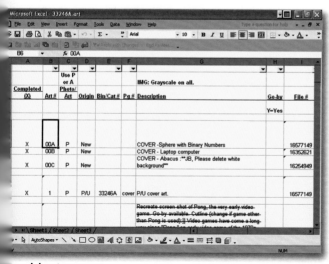

Spreadsheet program

Talent Release Form

I hereby assign and grant to the Boy Scouts of America the right and permission to use and publish the photographs/film/video tapes/electronic representations and/or sound recordings made of me this date by the Boy Scouts of America, and I hereby release the Boy Scouts of America from any and all liability from such use and publication.

I hereby authorize the reproduction, sale, copyright, exhibit, broadcast, electronic storage and/or distribution of said photographs/film/video tapes/electronic representations and/or sound recordings without limitation at the discretion of the Boy Scouts of America and I specifically waive any right to any compensation I may have for any of the foregoing.

PLEASE PRINT CLEARLY

Name:

Address:
(if under the age of 18)

Word-processing program

Word-processing software programs are tools that make writing—and formatting text—easier. Once words are typed into a document, they can easily be rearranged and corrected. Software may allow you to change the size and style (together, called the *font*) of the letters, as well as the color. You can easily align your paragraphs to the left, right, or center; add bullets or underlining; adjust the amount of indentation at the beginning of a paragraph, and alter the width of your margins.

Some programs let you add tables and graphics and will automatically number your pages. You can make different versions of your documents without completely retyping them, check your spelling, and produce neat printouts.

With the "mail merge" command, you can add names and addresses from a database program to a form letter you have written to send out to a large group—for example, to every Scout in your troop.

Database managers, spreadsheets, and word-processing programs usually come preinstalled on new PCs. If not, get programs bundled as an "office" or "productivity" suite—less expensive than buying separate programs.

sentation program

Application programs often come with templates, or sample files, already formatted and that may be very similar to the type of document you want to create. They also contain wizards, which are short programs that take you through the process of creating a new document step by step. Other programs come with a teaching aid called a tutorial that demonstrates the main features of the software. Use templates, wizards, and tutorials to save time and to learn how to use the programs as quickly as possible.

A popular aid for public speaking, a *presentation program* ows you to create screens or slides that list important points your speech, as well as pictures, charts, graphs, and even nds and animation. Slides you create can be projected onto creen in front of your audience, and can be advanced from e slide to the next while you speak. In addition, the text and phics portion of your presentation can be printed and tributed as handouts for your audience.

Desktop publishing programs allow you to design (or lay ou a page with a variety of elements, including words, pictures, and drawings. There are special tools for formatting text, suc as writing a headline in big, bold type; sizing images to fit yc layout; and adding color backgrounds, shading, boxes, lines, and other design elements. You can design a newsletter, a poster, or even a book using a desktop publishing program.

Graphics and design programs allow you to create and ec pictures and drawings on a computer. Paint or draw program create images in two dimensions. Other programs allow you to draw in two or three dimensions and create sophisticated models. These programs are known as *computer-aided design* or CAD, programs.

Photo-editing programs serve as a sort of digital darkroo helping you get the most out of digital photography. You can enhance pictures by cropping, sharpening, adjusting brightne and contrast, deepening color saturation, correcting color hue and otherwise improving your pictures. After all that "cosme surgery," you can print out photos or save them as digital file

Three-dimensional CAD programs can be used to creat **wireframes,** or outlines of objects, and **solid models,** which can show texture, light, and shadows. Automotiv engineers use CAD programs to design automobiles, down to each individual part.

A popular CAD software available for nonprofessionals is architecture programs that allow you to design rooms—even an entire house. You usually start by drawing the walls of the structure by dragging the cursor across the screen with your mouse, and the program automatically adds dimensions. You can place furniture in a room—using pull-down menus for couches, tables, etc.—and input exact measurements to match your own furniture.

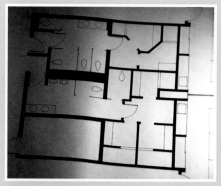

CAD architecture software allows the user to create a floor plan like this that can be printed out and shared.

Photo files can be saved at various *resolution* and *compression* levels, depending on how you will use the image. For printing, you want as high a resolution and as low a compression as possible, resulting in a large file size and sharp prints. For sending a photograph via e-mail, or for displaying a photo on a Web site, you want low resolution and high compression; this renders a small file size that will download to viewers' computers quickly.

Photo album programs help you organize your picture collection electronically on your hard drive or compact disc. This software may also let you create slideshows of your pictures that can be stored on a CD or DVD.

Video editing programs turn your computer into a digital movie studio, allowing you to edit and enhance video footage taken from a digital camcorder or converted from an analog camcorder. Simple forms of this software come bundled with digital video cameras and still cameras that have video capability, or you can buy more powerful video editing programs separately. The basic functions of these programs include cutting and rearranging video sections; adding transition effects, such as fades and wipes, between scenes; and adding titles and text, background music, and narration.

Most digital cameras come bundled with image editors.

Web page editors are programs that help you create Web sites without having to write HTML, the most common programming code used on the World Wide Web. Typically, these programs allow you to design your page—positioning text and graphics—by selecting commands from toolbars and icons. The editing program automatically creates the code needed. Most Web page editors also allow you to add advanced features such as animation and scrolling text. The programs also offer some help in "publishing" the Web pages you have created onto the Internet.

A related kind of software helps you create **blogs,** or Web logs, a special style of Web page that allows journal-like entries to appear, usually with the most recent at the top.

Financial programs help you keep track of your money. In their simplest form, they are like a checkbook that does all the addition and subtraction for you. Financial software has additional features that allow you to generate reports, helping you track how you spend your money by categorizing expenses (for example, entertainment, phone, school, and so on). It can also help you create a budget so that you won't overspend in particular categories. This kind of software can be linked to your bank account over the Internet so that you can update your check register automatically, and transfer funds between your checking and savings accounts.

Digital jukeboxes are programs that help you organize your music collection. You can use them to convert music from audio compact discs into files that can be stored on your computer. You can also add song files that you already own or have purchased. These programs allow you to create *playlists* of your favorite songs, "burn" songs onto CDs, and download your music files into portable music players. It is important to remember that copyrighted song files cannot legally be shared over the Internet (see "Copyrights and Piracy").

Communications programs allow you to connect to other computer users around the world and to millions of companies, schools, libraries, and individuals who maintain Web sites (see "The Internet and World Wide Web"). The connection software provided by your Internet service provider usually comes with an e-mail program for creating, sending, and saving e-mail, as well as an address book for storing e-mail addresses. It also usually offers a Web *browser* for viewing Web pages, or you can select another Web browser to run after your Internet connection is established.

It is important to protect your computer against malicious programs and intruders by using an antivirus program and a firewall, especially if you use the Internet via a high-speed or broadband connection.

Educational programs offer interactive training in such subjects as reading, mathematics, foreign languages, and test preparation. Rarely are these programs a substitute for a good human teacher, but they can offer useful practice and drills in the subject, like you might find in a workbook. Quality levels among educational software programs vary widely, so it is smart to read reviews of the products before buying one.

Since the early days of the Web, there have been small programs called "widgets" embedded in Web sites. Each widget is created by a small piece of programming code that can run in a Web browser. Early examples are simple counters, which show how many times a Web page has been loaded, or "hit." The use of widgets has exploded since then. Today there are thousands of different widgets, such as calculators, weather forecasts, airline flight information, and calendars. More exotic widgets include some that can translate text and others that stream radio or TV broadcasts to your computer. Widgets are also showing up on cellular phones and are increasingly being used in advertising.

Programming Languages

A *program* is a set of instructions that tells a computer how to accomplish a particular task. A programmer writes the instructions. A programming language is the tool that converts the programmer's instructions into a format that the computer can understand. There are dozens of programming languages—just as there are dozens of spoken languages—each filling a particular need.

Early programs were written in *machine code,* which is a series of 0s and 1s, the two numerals used in binary language. Machine code is the only language the computer's circuits can read. Each type of computer uses its own kind of machine code, so a program coded for one computer won't work on another type. A slightly more human-friendly code is *assembly language,* but it, too, is specific to a particular type of computer and is also considered low level.

As high-level languages were developed, programming languages became easier to create and understand because they consisted of English-like commands. However, a program written in a high-level language (sometimes called *source code*) must be "translated" or "compiled" into machine code before the computer can understand it. A *compiler* program converts the source code into machine code, also called *object code*.

```
0101000111000010101010001010101010101
1101101110010010001111110101101010101
1111010001011011011110001010111100111
0101110111000010111000001111010101010
0111110000101011001100111100101011110
0110001110101010111011101011010101010
0111110000110101010101011111010101011
```

Machine code is a low-level language that is hard for people to understand and very tedious to write.

Besides being easier for people to understand than machine code, a program written in a high-level language can have the advantage of being able to run on different computers. However, most commercial software products written for Windows and Macintosh computers are delivered already compiled as machine code, as 0s and 1s. That makes it harder for someone to study the code and figure out how it was designed. This helps companies like Microsoft and Apple protect their copyrighted products.

Here are early examples of *high-level programming languages*.

- COBOL (*C*ommon *B*usiness *O*riented *L*anguage) was popular for business-oriented data processing on larger computers. COBOL was designed for use by banks, utilities, manufacturers, government agencies, and other big operations.

- FORTRAN (*For*mula *Trans*lation) was one of the earliest programming languages, originally developed in the 1950s. Well-suited for mathematical calculations, FORTRAN was used primarily for scientific and engineering programming.

- BASIC (*B*eginner's *A*ll-purpose *S*ymbolic *I*nstruction *C*ode) was invented in the mid-1960s by two students at Dartmouth University in New Hampshire as an easy, all-purpose language for beginning programmers.

- Pascal, named after French mathematician **Blaise Pascal,** was originally designed as a teaching tool but is now often used in scientific programming, like FORTRAN.

- C is a very popular programming language because it was designed to work on many different computers. A program written in C for one type of computer can easily be converted to work on a different size or type of computer. C programs are still very popular for utilitarian embedded processors such as those used in fire alarm panels.

Object-oriented languages have become popular. Object programming is done by putting together groups, or modules, of commonly used commands—instructions on how to print, how to save information to a disk, and so on—into complete programs. Object programming saves time because the programmer can reuse parts of programs already developed by others. Called RAD, for Rapid Application Development, programming this way is more like putting together pieces of a puzzle than doing so from scratch. C++ was originally designed and implemented by **Bjarne Stroustrup,** currently head of the AT&T Large-Scale Programming Research Department. Originally known as "C with Classes," C++ was developed over a number of years beginning in the late 1970s, with a first standard certified in 1998. During this time, most graphical operating systems and major related programs were written with C++.

Delphi took the same kind of concepts and wrapped the older Pascal language within the development package. It combined the simplicity of a language similar to that used in Visual Basic with the power available with Visual C++.

Current development software from Microsoft includes NET versions of Visual C++ and Visual Basic. Also included is a newer language called C#. C# takes C++ a couple of steps further, and the language style is finding popularity with older Visual Basic, Visual C++, and Delphi programmers. Much of Windows Vista and Office 2007 were programmed in C#.

Meanwhile, C++ is still used by programmers for Apple's OS X and, even more so, the UNIX/Linux operating systems.

The popularity of the Web has spawned a generation of programming languages for building Web sites and performing computing operations over the Internet. The basic language for displaying text and pictures on Web sites and linking different Web pages together is HTML, short for *HyperText Markup Language*. It is simple to learn. To "soup up" a Web site by adding motion and interactivity, programmers use scripting languages such as Perl, Python, PHP, JavaScript, and VBScript.

Microsoft's Visual Basic became the most-used programming language for a number of years, with literally millions of Visual Basic programmers around the world.

With the growing use of animation and video on the Internet, more and more Web sites display content created with Flash, a multimedia platform with ActionScript, a scripting language. Flash is popular, in part, because it creates high-quality video and animations that are also compact, allowing streaming over the Internet quickly. Flash can also be made interactive, and is used to create Web site menus, animated games, and even tests and quizzes.

The Internet and the World Wide Web

Two or more computers working together can do far more than a single computer. When computers are linked, their connection is called a *network*. It might be a *local area network* (LAN), contained within a single building, or a wide-area network (WAN) covering a large region of the country.

These small and midsized networks, in turn, are linked to form a much larger system spanning Earth. That system is called the Internet. The Internet, simply stated, is a network of networks. When connected to the Internet, any computer can communicate with any other computer around the globe that is also connected to the Internet.

The amazing thing about the Internet is that it doesn't rely on any one central computer to operate, nor even a central network. No one organization controls it. Instead, the Internet operates across numerous high-speed networks maintained by various Internet service providers (ISPs) and private networks operated by different companies.

The Internet's origin can be traced to ARPANET, a small network launched in 1969 by the U.S. Department of Defense. ARPANET linked computers at various universities around the country. In 1974, researchers **Robert Kahn** and **Vinton Cerf** developed a way to join ARPANET with other similar networks; the networks were joined in 1983, and the Internet was born.

At first, all networks were connected to the Internet through a "backbone" network. ARPANET was the first backbone. Then came a high-speed network of supercomputers organized by the National Science Foundation. That backbone, in turn, was replaced by private high-speed networks in 1995. For years, only universities, military agencies, and defense contractors used the Internet. But as private companies were

There are billions of Web pages indexed on the World Wide Web—and an endless number possible.

allowed to join the Internet, and as local area networks started getting connected, it became possible for regular people to use the Internet, as well.

World Wide Web

As the Internet grew, a better way was needed to access and display the vast stores of information it held. That better way was the World Wide Web, first developed in 1990 by **Tim Berners-Lee,** a physicist at CERN, the European Particle Physics Laboratory. The Web—consisting of documents called Web pages—would eventually bring graphics, pictures, sound, animation, and video to the Internet. However, its true brilliance was in how it provided a simple system of organization.

One of Berners-Lee's two main innovations was the *URL* (Uniform Resource Locator), a form of address that can be used on any Web page or other file on the Internet. His other important invention was *HTML*, a form of computer language that creates Web pages that link to other Web pages through *hypertext.* A word in hypertext can be linked by way of a hidden URL to any other page, or part of a page, or file. Simply by clicking your cursor on the linked word, you can jump to some other location on the Internet, even if it is stored on a computer far distant from the page you started with.

To view Web pages, you need a software program called a *Web browser.* As Web pages add video, sound, and animation, additional software is needed to enable the browsers to use these multimedia elements. A helper software program "inserted" into a browser is referred to as a "plug-in." Widely used plug-ins are Flash and QuickTime, which allow a Web page to display video and animation. When videos are uploaded to a popular Web site (YouTube, for example), the video files, no matter what format they were created with, are converted into Flash files, which are compressed (made smaller) for easy loading onto a Web page.

Another kind of helper software used in Web browsers is called a *cookie*. A cookie is a small text file transferred to your computer from a Web site. The cookie, which contains information about you, such as your user name or shopping preferences, stays on your computer and is loaded into your Web browser the next time you visit the site.

Protocols and Domains

Every computer connected to the Internet can be identified by its unique Internet protocol address. A typical IP address looks like this: 345.18.99.248. Finding computers by their IP addresses was difficult, so in 1983, the University of Wisconsin created the domain name system (DNS), which allows you to find a computer on the Internet by a unique name connected to the IP address. (These names form part of the Web site's URL.)

Domain names, such as "www.scouting.org," always have two or more parts separated by dots. The part to the left of the top-level domain ("scouting" in this example) is the host name. The part of the name farthest to the right is the top-level domain, such as .com, .net, .org, .gov, and .edu. These letters alone can tell you something about the Web site.

• .com, .net, and .org—for general use

• .gov—reserved for governmental agencies

• .edu—for educational institutions, such as schools and colleges

Different countries have their own top-level domains; for example, .uk stands for United Kingdom, .au for Australia, and .ca for Canada. Web sites with those letters at the end are likely to be based in those countries. Once a particular domain name, such as www.boyslife.org, has been registered, no one else can use it. A nonprofit group called ICANN (the International Organization for Assigned Names and Numbers) maintains the Internet domain name system. ICANN regulates the buying and selling of domain names, which is handled by a number of private companies.

Web 2.0 and 3.0

There is already talk of Web 3.0, though the meaning of that term is not clear yet. Experts predict Web 3.0 will appear in the years 2010 to 2020 and will involve an even wider use of the Internet in our daily lives and may involve programs that use artificial intelligence.

In 2004, the term "Web 2.0" was coined. The 2.0 refers to a naming convention used to keep track of updated versions of software products (with the first version being 1.0, a slightly improved version being 1.1, 1.2, etc., and a major improvement being called 2.0). The term Web 2.0, however, doesn't refer to new technology, but rather the exploding variety of new ways that existing Web technology is being put to work. This variety is due largely to the widespread availability of broadband (high-speed) Internet connections. During the early days of the Web, people mostly used it to read information. In Web 2.0 people use the Web for shopping, social networking, sharing videos, writing blogs, watching television shows, and fostering collaboration in such projects as Wikipedia, the online encyclopedia maintained by the people who use it.

Instant Messaging, Texting, and Video Chatting

Computers have also made possible new forms of communication. You already know that e-mail allows you to send a written message to any other computer user in the world who has a computer that is connected to the Internet. Another form of computer-enabled communication is *instant messaging*. It involves two or more people communicating in "real time," or in the moment, usually via text.

It is also the ability to see whether a particular person is online and connected to make an instant messaging exchange

possible. So, you may be sitting at your computer in Omaha, Nebraska, while your friend sits at his computer in London, England. With instant messaging, a box comes up on both computer screens showing you and your friend that the other person is online. You type a message to him and he sees it instantly, then he types a response. If you have a camera attached to your computer, you could also stream video and audio back and forth. This so-called "video chatting" allows you and your friend to talk to each other and see each other, turning your computer into a sort of video telephone.

Another kind of instant messaging is *text messaging*, usually done through a cell phone, which contains computer chips. Texting is good for quick communication at times when phone calls might be disruptive or impractical, or when a person isn't available to take your call. Text messages can also be sent to order products or services, but you must be very careful not to receive unwanted charges on your cell-phone bill this way.

Search Engines

In 2008, the number of unique Web addresses (or Web pages) on the Internet surpassed one trillion! To find the information you need among all these pages, you use a *search engine,* such as the ones found at *google.com* or *yahoo.com*. Search engines use programs called *crawlers* to explore the Web and build indexes of Web pages.

To use a search engine, you simply type in your search term, for example, "history of the Internet," wait a moment, then see a list of Web pages pop up that contain the term you submitted. You can then click on any of the listed pages that you want to view.

If you use text messaging, be sure that you and your parent have a clear understanding of your using this special service. The costs associated with text messaging can be quite high.

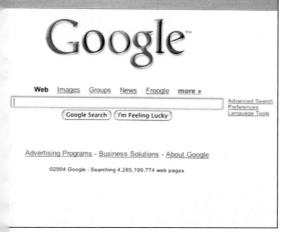

search engine like this one at www.google.com can help you locate information on the World Wide Web.

Tips for Online Safety

Protect Yourself

On the Internet, you can have fun, play games, and take care of business. You can find help with your hobbies and interests, learn all sorts of things, click your way to a wide world of instant information, and even read whole books. There are some risks that come along with the convenience of the Internet.

When you are online, you need to be careful to guard your privacy and protect yourself from potentially harmful situations. These tips will help you stay safe. Your parent, counselor, or librarian may talk with you about other rules for Internet safety.

1. Follow your family's rules for going online. Respect any limits on how long and how often you are allowed to be online and what sites you can visit. Do not visit areas that are off-limits. Just as there are places you don't go to in real life, there are places to avoid on the Internet.

2. Protect your privacy. Never exchange e-mails or give out personal information such as your phone number, your address, your last name, where you go to school, or where your parents work, without first asking your parent's permission. Do not send anyone your picture or any photographs unless you have your parent's permission.

3. Do not open e-mails or files you receive from people you don't know or trust. If you get something suspicious, trash it just as you would any other junk mail.

4. If you receive or discover any information that makes you uncomfortable, leave it and tell your parent. Do not respond to any message that is disturbing or hurtful.

5. Never agree to get together with someone you "meet" online, unless your parent approves of the meeting and goes with you.

6. Never share your Internet passwords with anyone (even if they sound "official") other than your parents or other responsible adults in your family.

7. Never shop online unless you have your parent's permission to do so.

8. Do not believe everything you see or read online. Along with lots of great information, the Internet has lots of junk. Learn to separate the useful from the worthless. Talk with your counselor or other experienced Web user about ways to tell the difference.

9. Be a good online citizen. Do not do anything that harms others or is against the law.

It is important to remember that no one controls what information is put onto the World Wide Web. Much of what you see posted there may be incorrect or only partially correct. You must always consider the source of the information to help you evaluate how accurate it might be.

Protect Your Computer

Besides taking precautions to protect your personal safety online, you should protect your computer from a number of online dangers, including malware and theft of files. *Malware* is a term covering several types of harmful files, including *viruses* (software code designed to harm your computer in some way, such as by destroying files or causing your computer to malfunction), *worms* (files that infect your computer and send out copies of themselves from your computer over the network), and **trojan horses** (programs that appear to do something useful but actually are harmful as well). Another form of malware is *spyware*. Such programs, often attached to some useful software, "spy" on you, tracking your movements on the Web. Spyware can also install secret programs on your computer. Your computer can catch a malware infection from an e-mail message, Web sites, or infected disks.

These tips will help you keep your computer safe. Your parent, counselor, or librarian may talk with you about other rules for avoiding viruses.

1. Look carefully at the return address of all e-mail messages that you receive, especially those that arrive with attachment. Only download a file from someone you trust; even then, be suspicious. Sometimes a virus can be sent from a friend computer without his knowledge if his computer is infected. Be particularly wary of a file attachment with a name ending with ".exe," which indicates an "executable" program file that may harm your system.

2. Install antivirus software on your computer and keep it updated. The software can be set to automatically look for viruses on your hard drive, to scan disks and files that you put into your computer, and to scan e-mail attachment that you receive.

3. Don't open e-mail that appears to be *spam*, or junk mail, which may only be trying to sell you something but could also introduce a virus into your computer.

4. Back up your important files regularly onto optical storage media (CDs, DVDs), flash drives, or extra hard drives. (There are also online backup services available for a yearly fee.) It is prudent to make your backup redundant; that is, back up to more than one type of media. Be sure to scan your backup media for malware, too.

5. Only buy software from trusted sources. Unauthorized copies of software programs often contain viruses and should be avoided.

6. For added protection, use a *firewall,* which can consist of software, hardware, or both, to keep intruders from looking at and possibly stealing private information stored on your hard drive, such as passwords or credit card numbers. Use of a firewall is particularly wise if you have a broadband connection to the Internet. The latest versions of Windows and Macintosh operating systems have built-in firewalls that you can activate to protect your computer online.

Newspaper and magazine publishers use computers to edit and design print produc
and online publications.

Computers at Work

Today, computer skills are useful in almost every position. As computer technology has become cheaper and more powerful, it has spread into practically all lines of work, from farming to medicine, from landscape design to aerospace.

Basic application programs—word processing, spreadsheets, etc.—are used throughout the economy. But beyond that, each industry uses specialized software, and often specialized computers, tailored for the specific needs of the profession.

Graphic designers and special-effects creators use computers to produce special film sequences for movies and television commercials.

Air-traffic controllers who guide commercial airplanes in and out of airports use sophisticated computer systems to help them do their jobs.

Music publishers record and edit music digitally using computer equipment.

Newspaper and magazine publishers use computers to edit and design print products and online publications.

Professional translators use computers to automatically translate writing from one language into another.

Doctors use computers to store and retrieve the medical records of their patients and to access medical information that can help them diagnose and treat illness.

Architects use computers to help them design buildings.

The computer industry itself is huge and offers many career opportunities:

- Electrical engineers design hardware.

- Electronics technicians build and repair it.

- Software engineers and computer programmers design and write new application software.

- Information technology managers develop and manage computer systems and servers for business, industry, government, science, and health care.

- Schools and universities need teachers and professors who can teach computer science.

Since the mid-1990s, the Internet has opened up an entirely new field of computer-related careers. Today, most companies maintain corporate Web sites, conduct business over the Internet (including billing and receiving payments), and market their products through Web advertising. These companies need technicians to maintain Web servers and e-mail servers, designers and graphic artists to design Web pages, programmers to code Web pages, and technology managers to keep operations running smoothly. Additionally, more companies are creating a presence on social networking sites, such as MySpace and Facebook, in order to better market their products. Most positions already require at least basic computer skills, and the need will only grow in the future.

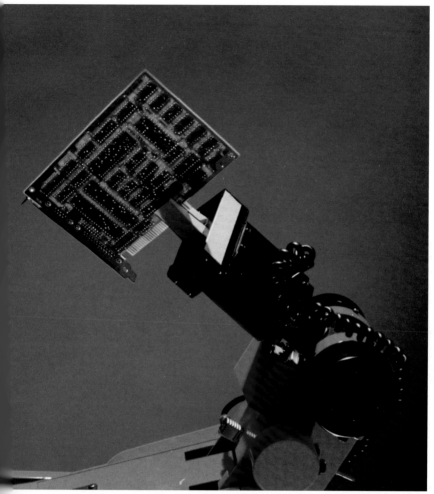

mputer-driven robots are used in manufacturing, where they provide precise
trol of sophisticated equipment.

Video Games: More Than Just Fun

The video game business, which today employs thousands of people, didn't exist before computers were invented. In just a couple of decades, it has grown from a small niche market to a major industry. In 2007, more than 267 million computer and video games were sold, or more than two games for every household in America. In the early days of video games, back in the late 1970s and early 1980s, many games were developed by one or two people working alone on their computers. Graphics were simple. Game play was crude and unsophisticated. Today, video and computer games are often large-scale productions involving entire teams of individuals working on different parts of the game.

Some of the types of workers employed in the video game industry include lead programmers, special-effects programmers, audio programmers, sound engineers, composers, art directors, game designers, level designers, graphic designers, screenwriters, producers, project managers, game testers, and business managers. Developing a game can take months of work and millions of dollars in costs. But the profits can be very high if the game is a success.

Recently, sales of computer and video games reached $9.5 billion per year in the U.S. alone, according to the Entertainment Software Association. Electronic games are played in 65 percent of American households. Responding to the demand, more than 200 colleges, universities, and design schools are now offering courses or even degree programs in game development and digital media; for a listing of such programs, see the Web site of the International Game Developers Association, *http://www.igda.org.*

Preparing for Your Visit

When you visit a business or industrial plant that uses computers, find out:

1. What type of computers are used—mainframes, minicomputers, workstations, personal computers, and so on.

2. What types of software programs are most useful to the company.

3. Whether any specialized software had to be written to meet the company's needs.

4. How many people work in the computer or information technology department of the business.

5. What kind of computer skills the company likes to see in new employees that they hire.

6. How the Internet and World Wide Web have changed the way the company does business. Ask whether the company has a corporate Web site and how many employees it takes to maintain the site. Ask if the company participates in social networking sites and whether it maintains a blog.

Copyrights and Piracy

When you draw a picture or write an essay, it belongs to you. It is a work resulting from your own creativity. Everyone has the right to control what he or she creates—whether it be photographs, writing, music, software, books, games, movies, or any number of other creative products. When you buy such a product, you don't actually own the content of that work. You own a copy of it. You have purchased the right, or *license*, to use that copy with certain restrictions.

Creative products and expressions of the human mind that have commercial value are called *intellectual property*. A digital music file or music CD, a photograph, a computer game, a movie DVD—these are examples of intellectual property. When you buy intellectual property, it is not like buying a pair of socks or a bookcase, which you can use in any way you want. Intellectual property is a special type of property protected by laws, including *copyright laws*.

One main restriction of copyright law is that you cannot make illegal copies of these works. Trading in illegal copies of copyrighted works is called *piracy*.

Unfortunately, computer technology has made it easy to make exact digital copies of certain kinds of intellectual property, including copyrighted software programs, games, music, photographs, books or articles, and movies. Compounding the problem is the illegal sharing of these pirated copies over the Internet through the use of file-sharing networks; these networks make piracy easy and seemingly secret.

The music industry loses $12.5 billion a year to piracy worldwide, according to the Recording Industry Association of America. When songs are pirated instead of sold legally, the record companies lose money. So do the artists who performed the music, the songwriters who wrote it, the store owners who sell it, and many other people who make their living bringing music to the public. According to industry estimates, more than 71,000 jobs are lost in the U.S. each year because of music piracy.

Not all copying is illegal. When you buy recorded music, you can usually copy it for your own personal use, say, in a portable music player. However, it is illegal to give copies of software or music to your friends. If you do, you are committing a crime. When you download pirated files into your computer, you also run the risk of downloading a virus that can harm your computer and data files.

There are legal ways to get music and software over the internet. Numerous online music stores make it easy to buy songs or entire albums for downloading over the Internet without breaking the law. There are also some Web sites, such as Pandora.com, that work like a jukebox or a radio station, allowing you to listen, legally, to music streamed over the internet. Streamed music is not downloaded or stored on your computer. Listening to streamed music is like listening to the radio, except that you have more choice over what you hear.

Likewise, some software, called *shareware,* can be downloaded or shared on a disk legally. Shareware is available at various Web sites, such as Download.com, and doesn't require you to pay for it before you use it. The people who make shareware want you to try the program and see if you like it. If you want to keep it, they ask you to pay for it by sending them money. Their name and address are usually displayed in the program.

Some publishers allow you to download a *trial version* of their software so you can try it out for a limited time. After the trial period is up, you must purchase the software if you want to continue using it or else the software will no longer work. Yet another type of software is called *freeware,* which you can download and use for free indefinitely. It is not copyrighted and can be used and copied.

In a recent year, software publishers lost more than $6.4 billion in the United States alone because of software piracy, according to a study by the Business Software Alliance.

Glossary

abacus. A counting device made of a series of beads on a frame.

analog. Describes a device or information that is continually variable, like a clock or a sound wave. The opposite of *digital*.

application software. Software or a program that is used to do specific tasks with a computer, such as writing or drawing pictures.

artificial intelligence. Making computers behave like humans, such as making decisions and understanding human language.

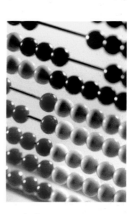

ASCII (American Standard Code for Information Interchange). A code made up of eight-bit characters that is understood by many different computers.

aspect ratio. The relative size of an image or computer screen, expressed as width by height. For example, a picture with a 2:1 aspect ratio is twice as wide as it is high.

BIOS (Basic Input-Output System). Built-in software that controls many basic functions of the computer, often stored in ROM or flash memory.

bit. Short for binary digit. The smallest possible unit of computer information. Each bit represents one switch in the computer that can be on or off.

bitmap. A grid on a computer screen made up of individual bits or pixels. The file name extension is ".bmp" and is a standard image format for personal computers.

blog. Short for "Web log." A Web site that acts like an online diary in which entries (text, photos, and videos) are usually posted in journal form, with the most recent at the top.

broadband. A transmission channel with high data capacity and high speed, able to carry video, audio, and data at the same time.

browser. A program that lets you find and explore information on the World Wide Web, including text, graphics, sound, and video.

byte. A binary character, consisting of eight bits of information which describes a letter or number.

client. Part of a client-server connection. The client is an application, such as an e-mail program, that runs on a personal computer. That computer is networked to another computer, called a server, which helps the client perform its work, such as sending an e-mail.

coaxial cable. A shielded wire used to transmit television signals, telephone calls, and high-speed (broadband) Internet.

CPU (central processing unit). The "brain" of the computer, where most of the calculations take place.

chip. A sliver of silicon used to hold transistors and other electronic parts.

circuit. The path of electric current that travels from the source of the power, such as a battery, through some device using electricity, such as a lightbulb, and back to the source.

compatible. Describes computers and software programs that can work together.

compiler. A program that decodes instructions written in an English-like language and then translates, or compiles, them into machine language.

compression. Shrinking a file. Compression can be lossless (preserving all the data in a file) or lossy in which some data is deleted.

computer. A system that processes and manipulates information.

cookie. A small file downloaded from a Web site to your computer to store information about your activity at the site, such as what items you placed in your "shopping cart" at a store Web site.

:oprocessor. A special chip that helps the nain "brain" of the computer to work faster t certain tasks, such as math or drawing.

:opyrighted. Describes written material, ncluding software, that is legally protected rom being copied or sold without the uthor's permission.

ursor. An indicator on a computer's monitor nat shows where the next character will go.

ata. Information.

atabase. A collection of pieces of information that fit together n some way, or have something in common.

atabase manager (DBM). Software that lets you keep track f information such as names, addresses, and telephone numbers.

esktop publishing. Describes programs used to produce ooks, newsletters, magazines, and other printed information sing a computer.

igital. Using numbers, usually binary, to perform, store, and splay a computer's calculations.

gital-analog converter. Circuits that allow analog information be converted to digital information (0s and 1s).

gital subscriber line (DSL). A high-speed (broadband) ternet connection delivered over a standard copper ephone line.

gitize. To change something such as a picture or a sound to a form that a computer can understand.

main name. The unique name that identifies an Internet site, vays written with two or more parts separated by a period.

wnload. Transferring information "down" from someone e's computer to one's own computer, by way of a local a network connection or the Internet.

ver. A small computer program that allows the computer communicate with a peripheral device, such as a printer scanner.

ctronic mail (or e-mail). A message sent from one person another using a computer or other electronic device.

extension. The suffix, or letters following the period in a file name, which identify the type of file named.

field. Part of a database in which a specific type of information is stored, such as telephone numbers.

firewall. Software or hardware that protects a computer or a private network of computers from other computers on the Internet.

FireWire. A fast, high-capacity port on a computer for transferring large amounts of data, such as video footage from a digital camcorder. Also known as IEEE 1394.

flash drive (or thumb drive). A compact storage device using flash memory that can be plugged into a computer's USB port.

flash memory. A rewriteable memory device, such as the memory chips that hold digital photos, that keeps its data even when power is turned off.

format. The particular manner in which data is stored.

freeware. Software that is not copyrighted and can be used and copied by anyone. Also known as public-domain software.

gigabyte (GB). One billion bytes or one thousand megabytes.

graphics program. A program used to create and edit pictures using a computer.

grayscale. How black-and-white images are represented on a computer screen, in individual pixels of different shades of gray.

hacker. A person who uses a computer illegally to sneak into other computers and steal or change information.

hard drive. A rigid disk consisting of several platters that store information in magnetic form, usually installed inside a computer.

HTML (HyperText Markup Language). The basic language for displaying text and pictures on Web sites and linking different Web pages together.

icon. A picture on the computer screen that helps you tell the computer what to do.

impact printer. A printer that strikes the paper through an inked ribbon to produce characters on the page.

ink-jet printer. A printer that sprays ink onto a page to produce characters.

input device. A device by which data can be entered into a computer.

integrated circuit. A group of related circuits all manufactured together in a single chip.

intellectual property. Ideas and expressions of the human mind considered unique and original and to be worth money in the marketplace—and deserving of protection under the law.

internet. A worldwide system of computer networks.

internet protocol (IP) address. The address of a computer on the Internet. Every computer connected to the Internet has an IP address, either a permanent one or a different one that is assigned to the computer each time it connects.

kilobyte (KB, or K). A little more than a thousand bytes of information—1,024, to be exact.

local area network. A computer network within a single office, building, or other site.

lossless/lossy. Compression can be lossless (preserving all the data in a file) or lossy, in which some data is deleted.

machine code. A programming language made up of sets of binary codes that a computer uses to pass instructions back and forth among its parts. Sometimes called *low-level code.*

magnetic memory. A means of storing data using magnetic particles, such as on a floppy disk, hard drives, or recording tape.

mainframe. A large, powerful computer.

malware. Damaging or "malicious" software intended to disrupt a network or a single computer. Types of malware include viruses, worms, and trojan horses.

megabyte (MB). One million bytes.

memory. Where a computer stores information, for example, in RAM or ROM, or on compact discs or hard drives.

microcomputer. A personal computer.

microprocessor. The "brain" of a microcomputer.

minicomputer. A midsized computer.

modem (MOdulator DEModulator). A device used by computers to communicate over telephone lines or television cables.

monitor. A computer screen.

motherboard. The main circuit board of a computer, which contains the central processing unit.

mouse. A movable device used to point to different locations on the screen and send signals to the computer.

network. A group of connected computers.

object code. Instructions for the computer that have been converted from English-like instructions (high-level code) into machine code (low-level code).

object-oriented programming. A programming technique that uses parts of existing programs, or miniprograms, to produce more complicated programs.

operating system. Software that allows the computer to perform basic functions.

optical storage. Technology that uses lasers to sort and retrieve information.

output device. Any device such as a monitor, printer, or sound card that allows you to send out information from a computer.

peripheral. An attachment to a computer, such as a printer or a mouse.

personal computer (PC). A small computer with software oriented toward easy, single-user applications. Often used to distinguish a microcomputer running a Windows operating system, as opposed to a Macintosh.

personal digital assistant. A handheld computer, commonly called a PDA, that can provide a range of basic computing functions.

piracy. Illegal copying, selling, or giving away of intellectual property.

pixel. Short for picture element. A single dot on a computer screen.

plotter. A printer that uses pens to draw on a page.

port. A place on a computer where accessories and peripherals can be plugged in and connected.

printer. A device used to print out information (usually on paper) stored in a computer.

program. A set of computer instructions.

programming language. The language used by a program to write instructions that a computer can understand or interpret.

protocol. The rules computers use to communicate with each other.

punched card. A paper card punched with hole patterns that was used to load information into early computers.

RAM (random-access memory). Temporary memory that the computer uses to store programs and information until the computer is turned off.

read. To retrieve information or a program from storage and put it into the computer's internal memory. The opposite of write.

resolution. Describes in how much detail an image is printed (in dots per inch, or DPI) or displayed on the computer monitor (a number of pixels wide by number of pixels high).

ROM (read-only memory). Permanent, unchangeable memory used to store basic instructions the computer needs in order to operate.

router. A device or software that serves as a bridge between two or more networks. A router determines the best route for sending a packet of data to its destination.

scanner. A device similar to a copier that changes a picture into digital information.

search engine. On the World Wide Web, a set of programs that seeks out information you request and presents you with an index of Web sites containing the information.

sector. An area on a disk where information is stored.

semiconductor. A material, such as silicon, that can both conduct and resist electricity.

sensor. A device used to convert physical information such as temperature, light, or electric current into data meaningful to a computer.

server. A computer on a network that manages shared resources, such as files or Web pages.

shareware. Software that you pay for after you have tried it and decided to use it.

software. Any computer program.

sound digitizer. A circuit that converts sound into digital form.

sound card. A set of chips on a board that includes a digitizer and allows a computer to produce or record sound.

source code. A program in a language prepared by a programmer that must be compiled into object code for a computer to understand it.

special-purpose computer. A computer designed for a specific purpose, such as controlling the antilock brakes of an automobile.

spreadsheet program. A program used to help solve math-oriented problems such as budgets.

spyware. Software installed on a computer without permission that sends information about the computer user over the Internet.

supercomputer. The fastest type of computer made.

tape drive. A storage mechanism that uses tape cartridges instead of disks.

template. A sample file of an application program already formatted to meet common needs, such as a business-style letter in a word-processing program.

terabyte. A thousand billion bytes, or a thousand gigabytes.

thermal printer. A printer that uses special heat-sensitive paper to produce an image.

third generation (3G). High-capacity wireless communications protocol that can transfer data over cell phones beyond just voice calls, for example, allowing you to watch TV on a cell phone.

tracks. A series of circles on a disk, like the rings of a bull's-eye, that store information.

transistor. A device that can both conduct and resist an electrical current, functioning as a switch.

Trojan horse. A virus or harmful computer program disguised to look like a useful program, such as a screensaver.

true color. The effect of the maximum amount of colors that can be produced by pixels.

upload. To transfer information from one's own computer "up" to someone else's computer via a local area network or the Internet.

USB (universal serial bus) port. The device used to connect all such peripheral devices. Another type of high-speed port FireWire.

Wi-Fi (wireless fidelity). A method of connecting computers in a network with radio signals rather than wires.

wizard. A short program, or utility, within application software that leads you through all the steps needed to accomplish a task.

word-processing program. A program used to prepare, store, display, and print text created on keyboard.

workstation. A networked computer typically more powerful than a personal computer.

World Wide Web. The collection of all the resources and users on the Internet that can be accessed with a Web browser.

worm. A software program that, once installed on a computer, copies itself and sends its copies over a network to infect other computers without permission.

write. To store information or a program. The opposite of read.

Computer Resources

Scouting Literature

Drafting, Electricity, Electronics, Engineering, Graphic Arts, and *Photography* merit badge pamphlets

Visit the Boy Scouts of America's official retail Web site at *http://www.scoutstuff.org* for a complete listing of all merit badge pamphlets and other helpful Scouting resources.

Books About Computers

Ceruzzi, Paul. *A History of Modern Computing.* MIT Press, 2003.

Farr, Michael. *Top 100 Computer and Technical Careers: Your Complete Guidebook to Major Jobs in Many Fields at All Training Levels.* Jist Publishing, 2008.

Gookin, Dan. *PCs for Dummies.* For Dummies, 2007.

Gralla, Preston. *How the Internet Works,* 8th ed. Que, 2006.

Kent, Steven. *The Ultimate History of Video Games: From Pong to Pokemon.* Three Rivers Press, 2001.

Kraynak, Joe. *The Complete Idiot's Guide to Computer Basics,* 4th ed. Alpha, 2007.

Miller, Michael. *Absolute Beginner's Guide to Computer Basics.* Que, 2007.

Reid, T.R. *The Chip: How Two Americans Invented the Microchip and Launched a Revolution.* Random House, 2001.

Rothman, Kevin F. *Coping With Dangers on the Internet.* Rosen Publishing Group Inc., 2000.

Sethi, Maneesh. *Game Programming f Teens.* Course Technology PTR, 200

Spraul, V. Anton. *Computer Science Made Simple.* Made Simple, 2005.

White, Ron. *How Computers Work,* 9th ed. Que, 2007.

Periodicals

Game Developer magazine
Web site: *http://www.gdmag.com*

Mac Life
Web site: *http://www.maclife.com*

Macworld
Web site: *http://www.macworld.com*

PC Magazine
Web site: *http://www.pcmag.com*

PC World
Web site: *http://www.pcworld.com*

Popular Science
Web site: *http://www.popsci.com*

Scientific American
Web site: *http://www.sciam.com*

Organizations and Web Sites

American Society for Engineering Education
Web sites: *http://www.asee.org*
http://www.engineeringk12.org

Blogger (free blogging site)
Web site: *http://www.blogger.com*

The Computer History Museum
Web site: *http://www.computerhistory.org*

The Computer Society
Web site: *http://www.computer.org*

Entertainment Software Association
Web site: *http://www.theesa.com*

GIMP (GNU Image Manipulation Program)
Web site: *http://www.gimp.org*

Google Sketchup (simple, free introductory program to computer-aided design)
Web site: *http://sketchup.google.com*

Google Tech Talks (videos)
Web site: *http://www.youtube.com/user/googletechtalks*

Institute of Electrical and Electronics Engineers
Web site: *http://www.ieee.org*

International Game Developers Association
Web site: *http://www.igda.org*

International Intellectual Property Alliance
Web site: *http://www.iipa.com*

LiveJournal (free blogging site)
Web site: *http://www.livejournal.com*

OpenOffice.org (free and open productivity suite)
Web site: *http://www.openoffice.org*

Paint.NET (free software for digital photo editing)
Web site: *http://www.getpaint.net*

Picasa (free photo editing program)
Web site: *http://picasa.google.com*

Recording Industry Association of America
Web site: *http://www.riaa.com*

U.S. Department of Labor
Bureau of Labor Statistics
Web site: *http://www.bls.gov*

For the entry on computer-related careers in the *Occupational Outlook Handbook*, see *http://www.bls.gov/oco/oco1002.htm*.

Webopedia
Web site: *http://www.webopedia.com*

Wikipedia
Web site: *http://www.wikipedia.org*

WordPress (free blogging site)
Web site: *http://www.wordpress.com*

World Wide Web Consortium
Web site: *http://www.w3c.org*

Acknowledgements

The Boy Scouts of America thanks Scott Stuckey for writing this updated edition of the *Computers* merit badge pamphlet. Mr. Stuckey is a senior editor at National Geographic Society and the former editor of *Boys' Life* magazine.

The BSA appreciates computer programming consultant and trainer David Liske, Ann Arbor, Michigan, for his assistance with developing revised requirements and reviewing text.

The BSA is grateful to the Components, Packaging, and Manufacturing Technology Society of the Institute of Electrical and Electronics Engineers, in particular longtime national Scout jamboree staff member Ralph W. Russell II, IEEE Precollege Education Coordinating Committee, for lending their time and expertise in previous editions of this merit badge pamphlet, which forms the basis for much of the new edition.

We appreciate the Quicklist Consulting Committee of the Association for Library Service to Children, a division of the American Library Association, for its assistance with updating the resources section of this merit badge pamphlet.

Photo and Illustration Credits

American Museum of Radio, courtesy —page 12 *(transistor radio)*

Apple Computer Inc., courtesy—page 12 *(Macintosh computer)*

Frank da Cruz, courtesy—page 14 *(bottom)*

Jupiterimages.com—cover *(diskette, green circuit board, connecting cables);* pages 5, 9, 10 *(top),* 12 *(abacus),* 14 *(top),* 21 *(left),* 22, 26–27, 30, 34, 35 *(top),* 38, 39 *(bottom),* 43–45 *(all),* 47–50 *(all),* 52, 59–60 *(both),* 66–70 *(all),* 75, 77, 79, 81, and 83–93 *(all)*

Library of Congress, Prints and Photographs Division, courtesy— pages 12 *(Babbage, Hollerith)* and 17

Microsoft Corporation Inc.—page 65

MIT Museum, courtesy—page 18 *(bottom)*

NASA, courtesy—page 21 *(right)*

Photos.com—cover *(abacus, mouse, black circuit board, laptop);* pages 7, 13, 20, 25, 28–29, 32, 35 *(bottom* 36, 37 *(bottom),* 41–42 *(all),* 46, 51 *(top),* 62, 73, 80, and 82

University of Pennsylvania, courtesy —page 19

Wikipedia.org, courtesy—pages 15 *(both),* 16, and 23 *(bottom)*

Wikipedia.org, courtesy (photo by Asim18)—page 39 *(top)*

Wikipedia.org, courtesy (photo by Rama)—page 23 *(top)*

All other photos not mentioned above are the property of or are protected b the Boy Scouts of America.

Brian Payne—page 76

Randy Piland—cover *(Scout);* pages 11 *(all)* and 78